MEET ME AT THE ICE CREAM

MEET ME AT THE ICE CREAM

New and Selected Poems

Sharon R. Chace

RESOURCE *Publications* • Eugene, Oregon

MEET ME AT THE ICE CREAM
New and Selected Poems

Copyright © 2021 Sharon R. Chace. All rights reserved. Except for brief quotations in critical publications or reviews, no part of this book may be reproduced in any manner without prior written permission from the publisher. Write: Permissions, Wipf and Stock Publishers, 199 W. 8th Ave., Suite 3, Eugene, OR 97401.

Resource Publications
An Imprint of Wipf and Stock Publishers
199 W. 8th Ave., Suite 3
Eugene, OR 97401

www.wipfandstock.com

PAPERBACK ISBN: 978-1-4982-9972-5
HARDCOVER ISBN: 978-1-4982-9974-9
EBOOK ISBN: 978-1-4982-9973-2

Lines from *The Indigo Bunting* by Vincent Sheean, quoting from Edna St. Vincent Millay's journals, reprinted courtesy of Holly Peppe, Literary Executor, Millay Society (millay.org).

New Revised Standard Version Bible, copyright © 1989 the Division of Christian Education of the National Council of the Churches of Christ in the United States of America. Used by permission. All rights reserved

SEPTEMBER 16, 2021

This book is dedicated to Ann Rogers, Walpole, New Hampshire native, and friend with our shared Rogers name. My maternal grandmother was Bessie Story Rogers of Rockport, Massachusetts. The Rogers family name is my middle name.

Contents

Acknowledgments | xi
Preface | xiii
Connecting the Dots | xiv

Creative Process

High Tea Jam | 3
Steps | 4
Art Class Sonnet | 5
Opening Creativity's Box | 6
Writing Life | 7
Aubade | 8
Throwing Out a Thesaurus | 9
Attendance Records | 10
Rotating the Tires | 11
Red Light—Green Light | 12
Poet's Horn Book | 14

Preserves

Butter | 19
Our Town in Three Precincts | 20
Web of Being | 22
Pitch | 23
Announcements | 24

Church Bell Blessing | 25
Bermuda Beatitude | 26
Assurance | 27
Wedding Poem | 28
Rockport Harbor | 29
April Blessing | 30
Mother's Day | 31
Memorial Day | 32
RE: 9/11 | 33
Fourth of July, 2016 | 34
Bird's View | 35
Sonnet for Sailors | 36
Cloudy Beach Day | 38
Bloom of the Sea | 39
Beauty Aglow | 40
Sonnet of Faith | 41
Creating Beauty in Community | 42
Rosemary's Garden | 43
Sustenance | 44
Magnification | 45
Uncertain Forecast | 47
Chipmunk Nervously Scampering | 48
Thirty-Two Inches of Snow in Gloucester | 49
Weather Event | 50
Sea Smoke | 51
Waves | 52
Chords | 53
Route 16—Tractor Supply | 54
Tabletop Tree | 55
Page Turner | 56
A Love Triolet | 57
Village Church | 58

Endnotes

Streaming Beauty | 63
Blue Heights | 65
Pandemic Peace | 67
Connection of Presence | 68
Witness | 69
Open Letter of Questions | 70
Pandemic Puzzle | 72
Japanese Gardens | 73
Distillation | 74
Dead Whale | 76
Moving On | 77
Lament and Praise | 78
A Memorial Poem | 79
Image of Life | 80
Fog | 81
Fog Repeats | 82
Completion | 83
Seasoning | 84
Shoots | 85
Intimations | 86
Sinatra Inspired | 87
Clothing and Callings | 89
Translation | 90
Meet Me | 91
Indigo Bunting Sonnet | 93
Blue Sonnet | 94
Goodwill Dawning | 95
Imperative | 96

APPENDIX A: *Padraic Colum Evokes Gratitude* | 97

Acknowledgments

Thank you to daughter Amy Elizabeth Chace for the cover art. I am grateful to Karen Barr Grossman for her editorial comments, her skill in formatting, and our weekly pandemic phone calls. Husband Ernest listened to many concerns on the journey to publication. Some poems were published in slightly different versions in *The Gloucester Daily Times* of Cape Ann, Massachusetts, and the *Record Journal* of Meriden, Connecticut. Gifts of publication helped me grow in purpose and confidence and poetry workshops led by James R. Scrimgeour, Professor Emeritus of Western Connecticut State University, offered literary refinement and companionship. My appointment as poet laureate of Rockport by the Board of Selectmen is a cherished honor.

Preface

DEAR READERS:

The unifying theme of my life and the poems in this book is sustaining beauty. I have always known that beauty is important to me but it has taken years to come to a fuller understanding. Sustaining beauty is beauty that nourishes individuals and communities. My high school idealism recorded in the 1962 Rockport High School year book, *Rocks and Pebbles*, states my youthful ambition: "To help make the world a better and more beautiful place."

A few years ago, my Albion College classmate Dorothy said that she remembered when I asked what sustains her. Whatever her answer was I have forgotten. Coffee and apple pie that we enjoyed together in an Albion coffee shop were nourishing for both of us that day. My response was that I was sustained by friends who understood and accepted that I lacked the physical stamina and coordination typical of other Albion College students. Their understanding gifted the social beauty of acceptance. My physical challenges and slow development likely caused by too much oxygen in a 1944 incubator were addressed much later. Because many people could not accept a disability I could not explain, I encountered judgmental and even cruel people who insisted I "could if I wanted to . . . " despite my smaller portion of stamina.

At the same time family members told me the story of the tortoise and the hare. Slow tortoise wins the race. Yes, I win, but not in competition with others, in competition with myself, to keep going in order to improve art and writing. People actually see me as energetic and powerful with words: it is ironic and thrilling for the weak child I was labeled. I certainly claim to be intellectually lively. My inability to drive a car has flabbergasted many, and conventional wisdom is that "if you just practiced more you could drive well." No, that is not who I am. Longer practice meant familiar fatigue taking over, and I drove more poorly with each mile of practice. Lacking the stamina and coordination of many others, I have to conserve strength to do the things I do best.

In 2018, fifty-two years after graduating from college, I wrote the following poem that is personal yet also branches out to other people in different circumstances. Openness to the sustenance of beauty may be a shared stance especially for people with loss as constant memory.

Connecting the Dots

Miss Munro, Albion English professor,
admired by numerous students,
was happy that I would see the Rosetta Stone.
The Rosetta Stone unsheathed language.
It was a stunning proof of a turning point,
a revolutionary change.

In Rockport . . . a half century
later, time to connect memories,
I saw the tiniest of daisies
gracing spring-green grass:
reminding me of dainty daisies
dotting London parks cherished
on that 1965 Albion College tour
when I saw the Rosetta Stone.
Daisies unlocked feelings, heart beats
struggling to blossom into words.
So for many years I felt guilty
that the daisies mattered more.

Years later, my friend, Fran, said that
on her trip the best part of London
was the tiny flowers in the grass.

Preface

"Others did not get it," she said.
Shared observation, hard for us
to explain sustaining beauty.

Fran and Sharon, Sharon and Fran
childhood friends bonded in art,
creating with pencils and paints,
once again partners in perspective:
Fran, slow to read, yet a strong swimmer,
Sharon, slow to learn to walk,
yet in her grandmother's words
"A poet but you do not know it."

The flowers are a gift of
gladness, giving strength
to transcend splintering forces
of marginalization in school
and shame in the family for being
frail and clumsy.
For Fran and me the rising
is personal.

Poems of self have global
dimensions . . . world poems,
contain many selves.
For Londoners, perhaps
the daisies were symbols of life
budding after World War II.
After recent subway bombings,
trust that shattered humanity
will flower again is fragile.
Yet daisies bloom in present hope
between memory and the future.
Take courage.

Preface

My poems as products are my preserves. The words "conserve" and "preserve" are related. Conserving energy aids poetry writing because I can ponder while resting and compose first drafts in my head. I consider my finished poems to be my preserves, the sweet jam that I write about in "High Tea Jam." In this book, poems about the creative process are like aromatic fruit simmering on the stove to make jelly. Poems in the section "Preserves" are as varied as the jams and jellies in the marketplace. Endnote poems are bittersweet like marmalade when they are about death. Yet the word "end" also suggests purpose, a thread woven into the endnote poems. The word "preserves" as a noun describes jam or jelly. As a verb, "preserve" means to protect from being lost. Poems as preservation of distilled experience offer company, comfort, challenge, and celebration.

Beauty that sustains comes in many forms including beauty in nature, communities of faith, lives well lived, shared interests, and civic engagement. Silence is for me a sacred kind of beauty. I invite you to look, listen, and linger with my poems. My wish is, dear readers, that you will glimpse beauty not only in my poems but, more importantly, in your lives.

Sincerely,
Sharon
November 2020

Creative Process

High Tea Jam

The confines of my life
serve to conserve strength.
Seeds sown in silent, stillness
swell then burst their hulls
and blossom into mind fruit.
Cherries of the soul simmer,
boil down into sweet preserve,
a foretaste, a bow to the
Eternal Now.

Portfolio of Painterly Poems: A Pilgrim's Path to God
Resource Publications, 2006
An Imprint of Wipf and Stock Publishers

Steps

At
age four
I had to
learn walking down
stairs so family
devised exercises.
Still at age ten, one step then
stop was slow going down the stairs
in the Pigeon Cove School where no one
would push me down. However I had to
plan well how to best maneuver and therefore
waited to go last or rushed to go first or squeezed
against the railing and wall so others could quickly pass by.
But I was excellent with crayons, bright, bold, beckoning.

Art Class Sonnet

Art class the warm summer when I turned nine,
By lovely Evelyn Longley taught
I rode the bus from Pigeon Cove each time
Favorite days when colors all I sought.
Sunshine, white clouds and Motif #One
Rockport icon drawn, painted carefully.
My word-free, arty world had just begun
Line, love, texture ahead applied fully.
Mixed blue and white made perfect, summer sky
To remember on future, foggy days.
In time, too soon, we had to say *Goodbye*.
Color memories keep sadness at bay.
There is present sense of eternal time.
Art goes on—creative process assigned.

Portfolio of Painterly Poems: A Pilgrim's Path to God
Resource Publications, 2006
An Imprint of Wipf and Stock Publishers

Opening Creativity's Box

Picture this, 1954:
Fresh cardboard scent,
a red mini-chest with a
flap that snapped shut,
over-the-top tray filled
with pencils and eraser,
the bottom drawer
with a six-inch ruler,
compass and protractor,
suggested compartments
of knowledge in fifth grade!

Fast forward to 1964:
Math and rulers were not
my tools nor treasures.
But the shape inside
the protractor became
rhythm and design
on a leather tile created
for Art Composition 204.

In time, fifty-two years later,
this poem—first draft in pencil.

Writing Life

Brownies likely
when blessed by friends who come to tea.
Cups of warmth, doily daintiness
lighten aubades and sweeten nocturnes.

When blessed by friends who come to tea,
continuing conversations
lighten aubades and sweeten nocturnes.
Finger foods strengthen hearts for work.

Continuing conversations,
cups of warmth, doily daintiness,
finger foods strengthen hearts for work.
Brownies likely.

Cape Ann and Beyond the Cut Bridge: Culling and Cart-wheeling
Resource Publications, 2015
An Imprint of Wipf and Stock Publishers

Aubade

Morning light filters through
drawn draperies, the color and
texture of pared parsnips.
Harvey, our orange and white,
butterscotch sundae cat, pokes
his nose through the opening
and looks out the window.
Is there a good poem here?
No, not really. Dawned on me.
Not every scrap needs to be saved,
nor every fragment fashioned into
art. Some observations are simply
to enjoy. Like cats.

Portfolio of Painterly Poems: A Pilgrim's Path to God
Resource Publications, 2006
An Imprint of Wipf and Stock Publishers

Throwing Out a Thesaurus

I tossed my thesaurus, old friend,
worn out, falling apart, yet loved
high school graduation present
in 1962 from my second mother,
lover of words, Rockport author.

You served me well,
Mr. Roget, and still do
in a slightly newer version,
found for free in the Book Barn,
at our town's Transfer Station.
(AKA Dump)

I do not expect to find *WiFi*
or an electronic meaning
of *tablet*. Instead I'll search
for nuances of integrity,
kindness, graciousness,
family, affinity, and divinity.

Attendance Records

Beach parking stickers
In rows on back windows
Like Baptist Sunday School pins
Circa 1950, Okay, Okay—
Other churches, too.

It takes miles of beach walking,
Looking, pondering, picking up
Shells, beach glass, blue and white
Pieces of Delft matching the colors
Of the day to craft a word picture,
A phrase of feeling, beauty savored.

Going back a long way,
My best distilled line—
The incense of kelp and iodine.
Breathing in salt air, joy continues.

Rotating the Tires

A Dialectic

1

Snippets spoke in sleep.
In a dream, my daughter
Amy and her friend, Holly,
about age ten, before boys set in,
felt called to help the neighbors
whose bicycles in unlocked garages
had tires going flat, needing rotation.

So they rushed into open doors,
and spun the tires around
as if twirling would prevent
life cycles, endless routines,
repetitions forever the same
deflating into the dullness
that maims.

2

Yet all households are not
exactly the same.
Cannot routines maintain
poetic time to dig like
archeologists, to excavate
interior mines, to find ancient
treasures in the mind?

Dearest Friends,
I end with good wishes
that your dreams evoke
yoked purpose and power
to twirl and pedal on.

Red Light—Green Light

Having lived in
two towns without
traffic lights, I much
prefer these tiny towns,
appreciate the implied
command to use your
own brain.

Traffic lights are not
always mechanical.
Intervals of time echo
the poetic rhythm of
create and rest, reflecting
first light in the beginning.

Caring people signal go,
proceed with caution,
or STOP. Wise directives
suggest idle intervals to rest,
then fuel and fire up engines
that drive work. Words flow.

When working on overdrive
to write a report comparing
the treatment of Vatican II by
The Christian Century and
Commonweal, a Jesuit professor
said: "Remember it is just a paper."

A stop sign was a gift
acknowledging hard work.
Grace from understanding that
breaks safe-guard proceeds.

In due time, a red light turned to green.

Poet's Horn Book

A. Anchor your craft in your inner harbor.

B. Brevity zooms to essence.

C. Consider, consider, consider.

D. Details create believability.

E. Embrace life. Give empathy.

F. Feel the beat. Follow the rhythm.

G. Guard against whining.

H. Haiku captures moments of fresh sightings.

I. Imagine, imagine, imagine.

J. Just keep going.

K. Know yourself.

L. Light, love, lift.

M. Mystery and meanings matter.

N. Night darkness brings out starlight.

O. Oh! The wonder of writing well.

P. Poetry gives form to distilled experience.

Q. Quilt the pieces together.

R. Reach, stretch, and grow.

S. Sonnets force an economy of words.

T. Trust in your creative process.

U. Underneath are deep, down things.

V. Value stillness.

W. Wonder is sacred.

X. Xenoliths are like interior treasures.

Y. Yearnings invite transcendence.

Z. Zippers that stick are part of life.

Preserves

Butter

Butter

Butter

Butter

Butter

Butter

Butter

Butter

S p r e a d

Inspired by
Concrete Poetry: Words and Sounds in Graphic Space
March 28–July 30, 2017, GETTY RESEARCH INSTITUTE

Our Town in Three Precincts

Precinct I
Petite Ode to Pigeon Cove

Sunken, magical tide pool
In the rocks of Pigeon Cove
Starfish, seaweed, shadows cool.
Cast in beauty's mold.

Lady slippers, pussy willows, rich dark loam,
In the woods of childhood memory,
Mystery as deep as a Buddhist koan.
Cast in beauty's chemistry.

Indigo buntings perch on telephone wires.
Tool Company turned to rust.
Joy flows, listening to all birds' choirs.
Cast in beauty's muster.

Precinct II
Rockport Triolet

Harbormasters are seaworthy.
Rockport boats rest in the harbor.
Even when winds are easterly.
Harbormasters are seaworthy.
Fog, rocks, waves are gray and pearly.
Ebb and flow feed like a larder.
Harbormasters are seaworthy.
Rockport boats rest in the harbor.

Precinct III

View from Old Garden Beach

All the pretty sailboats
With spinnakers blooming
Lady slippers of the sea
Brighten fog looming.

Web of Being

Neon orange flowing into pink,
the sunrise envelops the neighborhood.

Soft, glowing light is caressing,
yet the atmosphere does not care.

Beauty is the meeting ground,
announcing transcendence.

Signs of the matrix of goodness
shine in neighbors.

In the sweet faces of children
who live across the street.

In the determination of the older woman
who walks down the road each day.

In cheer from the mailman,
who delivers letters and good will.

Even in five wild turkeys,
like people seeking daily bread.

Pitch

Rosemary smiled with a mother-in-law's pride
when friends at the Sandy Bay Historical Society
rejoiced in the beauty of daffodils planted
by Bridgit at 25 Granite Street. "Stay tuned
for tulips," she said.

Stay tuned indeed.

Stay tuned for the Memorial Day Parade
with drummers beating in time throughout Time.
Stay tuned for the warm breezes of June
that feel like angels' kisses, for sand
between your toes in August, for the deepening
blue sea in September, for green gingko leaves
turning yellow in front of a former bank.
Stay tuned for the Christmas tree in Dock Square,
for all winter ducks and First Night.

Stay tuned.

A slightly different version was published in:
Cape Ann and Beyond the Cut Bridge: Culling and Cart-wheeling.
Resource Publications, 2015.
An Imprint of Wipf and Stock Publishers

Announcements

The internet gives speed
to carriers on the Cape Ann
information highway.

Glad to hear a lost
kitten is found, that
a coyote choir sang
at eventide.

An amorous skunk
announced with scent
that spring is here like
the biblical poet of love
proclaiming:

"For now the winter is past,
The rain is over and gone.
The flowers appear on the earth;
the time of singing has come,
and the voice of the turtledove
is heard in our land."*

---

* Song of Solomon 2:11–12

Church Bell Blessing

The new church bell rings sweet and clear.
Repaired steeple connects earth and heaven,
The mundane and the holy held dear.
Puritan past is shame yet also leaven.
Covenanted still to walk in godly ways together,
Welcome and inclusion replace heresy trials forever,
This sweeter note, hearts and minds will not sever.

Writing about the repaired steeple of the First Congregational Church, United Church of Christ in Rockport, Massachusetts, I was inspired by the book, *Mistress Bradstreet: The Untold Life of America's First Poet*, by Charlotte Gordon. I am grateful for publication in *The Gloucester Daily Times*, issue of August 24, 2018. It is an homage to Anne Bradstreet, using the rhyme scheme she created: ababccc.

Bermuda Beatitude

2017

Swimming with dolphins on Sunday,
Grandmother dolphin understands
That I swim slowly . . . feeling
Bermuda blessing, deeper than church.

Grandmother dolphin understands
More than most people know,
Bermuda blessing, deeper than church,
Dolphin devotion, nature's sacrament.

More than most people know
I swim slowly . . . feeling
Dolphin devotion, nature's sacrament
Swimming with dolphins on Sunday.

Thank you, Grandmother Dolphin, Cirrus.

Sincerely,
Sharon

Assurance

Evening primrose blooms
from dusk to dawn.

Purest lemon yellow
this lady of the night adorns.

Not afraid of darkness
at daybreak flowers rest.

Trusting on the roadside
is mighty blessedness.

Wedding Poem

August 1, 2015

Amy Elizabeth Chace to Paul Benincasa

Paul and Amy, Amy and Paul,
friends, lovers, parents, artists,
blessed by the covenant that binds,
married on bright day of black-eyed Susans.

Friends, lovers, parents, artists,
daughter in art, son-in-law of fine drawn line,
married on bright day of black-eyed Susans,
blooming together, growing into the future.

Daughter in art, son-in-law of fine drawn line,
blessed by the covenant that binds,
blooming together, growing into the future,
Paul and Amy, Amy and Paul.

Love,
Mom

Rockport Harbor

Haiku seaside scape:
Little waves of memories,
tribute to Rockport.

Rockport Harbor: Place
of work and wonder, busy
summers, winter storms.

A fleet of mallard
ducks sail across South Basin,
full tide of snow moon.

Lonely harbor swan
without your mate, sad years now,
people empathize.

Perfectly stitched, patch-
work quilt: Seamed breakwater gives
Rockport protection.

Full moon still shines in
the morning, luminous white
as snow coming soon.

April Blessing

Robin in the snow,
I wonder if you know
the joy you bring
when you sing of spring.
Pecking through the
crusty ice, you evoke
in me fresh zest for life.
When nature and grace
converge
Beauty is the Word.

Portfolio of Painterly Poems: A Pilgrim's Path to God.
Resource Publications, 2006
An Imprint of Wipf and Stock Publishers

Mother's Day

On Mother's Day
in 2014, the sun
is out in every
New England
zip code.
Warming our rocky shore
soft, breezes are
high contrast with
Puritan heritage, like
granite and wildflowers.
Some days are for stoic
endurance and others for
gathering wild roses.

Memorial Day

2015

1
The year of the perfect lilacs,
not past prime nor barely in bud,
florets form with scent borne
through nature's priestly
blessing, a balm of Gilead
soothing wounded warriors,
scarred by battles and bullets
and torn persons worn by
inner conflicts, deployed at large.

2
At the start of their school years
children march together
with flags and lilacs.
Drumbeats evoke transcendent
meanings in pondering minds.
Yearnings for healing peace
pulsate, pulsate, pulsate.

3
Hopeful parents take snapshots,
snippets of perfection or close
enough. Their digital pictures
to date, take little tablet space
with future fates unknown.
In time, images will transfer
to who knows where?

RE: 9/11

Spring, 2002

Nine months of silence,
another serious ring forms
around my somber core.
Thoughts form.
Word is born again.
September shadows are
the darkest of the year.
Following 9/11, words
within break forth.
A familiar hymn rises
through accumulated
debris in memory.
"The darkness deepens.
Lord, with me abide."

Portfolio of Painterly Poems: A Pilgrim's Path to God
Resource Publications, 2006
An Imprint of Wipf and Stock Publishers

Fourth of July, 2016

For Bill Elwell

"Good to see you," said Ernie.
"Glad to be seen," replied Bill.
Heart strengthened, happy each day,
Like his father, years passed.

"Glad to be seen," replied Bill.
Gladness also for firefighters, scouts,
Like his father, years passed,
Building church and community.

Gladness also for firefighters, scouts,
Heart strengthened, happy each day,
Building church and community,
"Good to see you," said Ernie.

Bird's View

For Nan Blue

Before the empty nest was blown away,
Nan, my friend and friend of birds,
noticed the ocean view from the nest,
more important than the safety of brambles.

Nan, my friend and friend of birds,
paused to wonder, walking with her dogs,
more important than the safety of brambles
broad horizon of Sandy Bay.

Paused to wonder, walking with her dogs,
noticed the ocean view from the nest,
broad horizon of Sandy Bay
before the empty nest was blown away.

Introduction: I met my older friend the late Laura Willhite in the Meriden Poetry Society of Meriden, Connecticut. Laura happily accepted my offer to toss a memorial bottle into the Atlantic Ocean off Cape Ann in honor of her late husband after Ernie and I returned to Rockport. I did not launch the bottle. More appropriately a naval seaman did. My poem "Sonnet for Sailors" summarizes the story and a postscript tells the rest of the tale.

Sonnet for Sailors

Arnold B. Willhite veteran mourned,
Pearl Harbor, submarines, saw Treaty signed.
While comrades gave tribute, my idea was born.
a memorial bottle hearts to bind.
"Laura, a message off Cape Ann?" I asked.
"Will be fun. Scotland bound?" Children agreed.
Harbormaster Rosemary joined in task.
Billy Lee offered to take it to sea.
Then United States Navy came to town,
USS *Boone* anchored in Sandy Bay.
Commander Evans's crew with plan most sound
launched bottle in Gulf Stream on its wavy way.
Meriden to Rockport, Gulf Stream water,
Scotland's coast through Navy's goodwill porter.

Postscript: On May 17, 2008, Andre Azevedo found the bottle while walking on Vila Cha Beach near Vila do Conde, north of Oporto, Portugal. Delfim Trancoso wrote to me on behalf of Andre and friends, who have a favorite scuba diving spot which is around a sunken WWII German submarine *U-1277*. The friends wrote a touching letter to Laura. Because they understand submarines and the life that Arnold "Jack" lived, they believe that they were meant to find the bottle. Portugal turned out to be a more significant place to beach than Scotland. I hope that someday the scuba diving friends will be able to visit Cape Ann.

Cape Ann and Beyond the Cut Bridge: Culling and Cart-wheeling
Resource Publications, 2015
An Imprint of Wipf and Stock Publishers

Cloudy Beach Day

Hazy horizon gently
defines blue-gray sky
touching purple-gray
brine.
Then fog fades even
shades of graphite.
Embracing breezes boost
the salt of the sea.
Soft mist gives seaweed
deeper hue. Overcast
matches my inner view.

Fog and fleecy
sweatshirts comfort
those of somber soul
wrapped in love
not seared by sun,
society's idol of
ceaseless demand
for smiley faces
drawn upon sand.

Portfolio of Painterly Poems: A Pilgrim's Path to God
Resource Publications, 2006
An Imprint of Wipf and Stock Publishers

Bloom of the Sea

The beach sweet pea
like laundry on the line
absorbs sunshine and fresh air,
spiced with salt.

Sandblasted lady of the beach,
dresses in lavender-blue.

Beauty Aglow

That time of pink sedum
before florets turn to russet
rose hips glow orange like
Jesuit and Wesleyan warmth.

Before rose hips turn to russet
days of discerning full bloom,
Jesuit and Wesleyan warmth,
inward turn, service bent.

Days of discerning full bloom
rose hips glow orange like
inward turn, service bent
that time of pink sedum.

Sonnet of Faith

Frost is on the pumpkin and the Prius.
Hydrangea blues have turned to pinkish plum.
New England calls the whole world to see us
purple asters, white, yellow, orange mums.
Stonewalls, straight paths signal hard knowledge
of coming winter, snow, sleet, graying days.
Stewing time in pots and minds will polish.
Writing song; art seeds thoughts for warming May.
Horizons dimmed by fog and northeast gales,
yet rose-pink and amethyst light the sky.
Take up your best: Imagine, forward sail.
Keep on. Persist. Grown strong. Inwardly fly.
Sunlight breaks through. Kiss peace with golden mist
resurrecting courage to bless, then risk.

Cape Ann and Beyond the Cut Bridge: Culling and Cart-wheeling
Resource Publications, 2015
An Imprint of Wipf and Stock Publishers

Creating Beauty in Community

"Oh, no. Now, I lost my special bracelet!"

"Hello, this is Sharon Chace of Rockport.
I'm hoping that someone found my bracelet."

"We are here to help. Can you describe it?"

"Yes. It is a line design, about six
and three quarters inches of very light
blue topaz and looks like aquamarine."

"We have it and will keep it here for you."
Thank you, Market Basket Associates
and customers on Cape Ann, island home.
I honor you with my iambic lines.

You have given me a feel-good story
to share, so feel proud of all of you who
are honest and true, creating beauty.
Husband Ernie bought me this blue bracelet
years ago. We weren't looking for it.
Caught our eyes, as we walked by a display.
A few weeks before our purchase, I had
a dream of one like it, stones in silver.
In that nighttime vision, I wore it to
celebrate the acceptance of a book
of poetry. Bracelet and book came true

Rosemary's Garden

Rosemary's garden flows
Lilacs, Rose of Sharon, Montauk daisies,
Throughout the seasons and the years.
Gifts of purple, blue, and white.

Lilacs, Rose of Sharon, Montauk daisies,
Beauty to share and bless,
Gifts of purple, blue, and white,
Loving links to cherished memories.

Beauty to share and bless,
Throughout the seasons and the years,
Loving links to cherished memories
Rosemary's garden flows.

Sustenance

The high school lad,
almost a Navy man,
held the ocean in his
vision.

When school lunch
was shepherd's pie,
and he had the money,
he bought two.

Hearty and basic as
service and salt air.

Magnification

Christmas 1952
Forty miles north of Boston,
an eight-year-old girl opens
her present and finds a
microscope promising 100,
200 and 300 powers of
magnification.
She thinks about the thread
and feathers that she will
examine more closely.
She smiles with wonder.

Twenty miles south of Boston,
an eight-year old boy opens
his present and finds a
microscope assuring 100,
200 and 300 powers of
magnification.
He thinks about the worms and
insect wings that he will
look at more closely.
He smiles with wonder.

Thirteen years later, boy
meets girl at the seminary
on the hill, the institutional
legacy of John Winthrop's
yearning for a Citty* upon a Hill.
Dust covers old prisms.

* Seventeenth-century spelling.

Ancient lenses break apart as
post modernism encroaches.

Lenses change. Polished
beacons light new paths.
The boy and girl, now a man
and woman, look through
the lens of historical criticism
and see how the situation in life
magnifies the importance of
discovering the original
meanings of sacred texts.
Through the lens of epistemology,
they consider the expanding role
of language, standpoints, and
attitudes in ability to learn.

Microscopic glass slides shift.
The lens of love magnifies
new meanings.
Ernie and Sharon smile with
wonder.

Cape Ann and Beyond the Cut Bridge: Culling and Cart-wheeling
Resource Publications, 2015
An Imprint of Wipf and Stock Publishers

Uncertain Forecast

Counter-melody to William Carlos Williams

Before the storm,
the snow plow,
in the driveway
next door, with
a yellow scoop
facing the road
waits.
Memories of winters
past drift back.
The future waits.
The plow and that
"red wheelbarrow"
compete.
So much depends
upon the DPW.

Cape Ann and Beyond the Cut Bridge: Culling and Cart-wheeling
Resource Publications, 2015
An Imprint of Wipf and Stock Publishers

Chipmunk Nervously Scampering

When the chipmunk scampers
along the stone wall and the
first orange leaf falls to the lawn,
the breeze is music for the dance.

Montauk daisies in scalloped
edged tutus stretch in arabesque.
The chipmunk pirouettes and leaps off
the wall to dig her burrow in the still
fresh grass. Summer green will not
forever last.

Pellet stove smoke is in the air.
The wind says, "Chipmunks, notice
the swirling milkweed seeds. Gather
quickly for your cache."
Swaying chocolate drop centers of
wilted black-eyed Susans will soon
have frosty, marshmallow toppings.

Standing on the highest stone in the
wall, the chipmunk stares as if
pondering rhythm. Inside it is
time to put the kettle on, gaze at
the fire, and join the dance to wonder.

Thirty-Two Inches of Snow in Gloucester

January 26, 2015

"Just another snow storm," said the guy from New Hampshire.
Stores ran low on milk and onions.
People want to make clam chowder, the white kind.
Winter is the time to hunker down in New England.

Stores ran low on milk and onions.
Rockport's breakwater held: Scituate turned off power.
Winter is the time to hunker down in New England.
Marshfield homes encased in ice: Flooding loomed at large.

Rockport's breakwater held: Scituate turned off power.
People want to make clam chowder, the white kind.
Marshfield homes encased in ice: Flooding loomed at large.
"Just another snow storm," said the guy from New Hampshire.

Weather Event

January, 2018

Rockport is featured
on the weather channel.
High tides, super moon,
winter storm named Grayson,
son of gray and sire of floods,
waves wash over T Wharf.

Scituate harbormaster overboard
is pulled to safety by a friend.
A college classmate calls to see
if we are sheltered in place.

Expect delays on the train lines.
Expect delays, a stormy haul to
reversing climate change.
Expect delays.

Sea Smoke

February 14, 2016

Sea smoke puffs rise
connecting sea and sky,
bridge to astonishment,
ineffable as mystical union.

Connecting sea and sky,
yearnings for transcendence,
ineffable as mystical union,
gift of nature and grace.

Yearnings for transcendence,
bridge to astonishment,
gift of nature and grace,
sea smoke puffs rise.

Waves

A wave of the ocean,
The swell of the sea.

A wave of feelings on Memorial Day,
Memories of waves suddenly rising.

A wave from a walking friend,
Sidewalk greetings of good cheer.

A wave of community's kind regards,
Warm wishes keeping well-being afloat.

Like Lucy Larcom, nineteenth-century New England poet, I have been troubled by yearning for the mountains while living in beauty with ocean views. In writing this poem, I discovered that love of two places offers the strength of harmony.

Chords

Ascent of the mountains
wideness of the sea,
pine boughs and beach roses
sing fragrantly to me.

Mountains in the springtime
summer by the sea,
New England notes crescendo
in chords of harmony.

Route 16—Tractor Supply

John Deere tractors
in signature green
are an army lined up
in rows, ready to go
into battle on rocky,
New Hampshire fields.

Plow and plant
pastures and dreams
savor being in
granite state beauty,
May Sarton pared to
"mountain, meadow, bird."*

---

* Allusion to May Sarton's poem, "As Does New Hampshire."

Tabletop Tree

Tiny tree,
You are a present
received with gratitude
for saving a little fir
in the woods.

White lights shine
through your pilgrim's
scallop shells glowing
on outstretched branches,
like the Virgin Mary's
arms of loving welcome,
on a white, marble
statue in a churchyard,
a cormorant drying wings
in the ocean breeze,
a child embracing joy
in the world.

Page Turner

Christmas, 2008
811.08, a Dewey decimal number,
angel's note in perfect pitch,
announces the promise of poetry.
Ernest gives me a dust jacketed,
discarded library copy of May Sarton's
As Does New Hampshire.
Her autograph, hidden we think, from
the bookseller is endowment of
surprising joy.

Unlike Eudora Welty who insisted
on conventionally autographing
the title page, Ms. Sarton in a
defining moment signed the
blank half-title page.
Black on white, stark as a crow on
pristine snow, less irritably iconic
yet intently independent in the
spirit of the state's license plate
intoning *Live Free or Die* . . . .
May Sarton chose her own page
as does New Hampshire.

Cape Ann and Beyond the Cut Bridge: Culling and Cart-wheeling
Resource Publications, 2015
An Imprint of Wipf and Stock Publishers

A Love Triolet

In New Hampshire a slice of love,
David said, "Nancy, buy the blouse."
Mud season yields to turtledoves.

In New Hampshire a slice of love,
"You are an angel from above,
Making for us a warm, clean house."
In New Hampshire, a slice of love,
David said, "Nancy, buy the blouse."

Author's Note: I remember this 1970 story because I was touched by Nancy's feeling that the Women's Fellowship was so special she wanted a new blouse to wear to a meeting. Equally impressed by David's empathy, I want to preserve this sweet remembrance.

Cape Ann and Beyond the Cut Bridge: Culling and Cart-wheeling
Resource Publications, 2015
An Imprint of Wipf and Stock Publishers

The pharmacist in this poem really did put a sign into a snow bank in front of his house reading SNOW FOR SALE. Dry humor for wet, snowy days!

Village Church

Snow piled five feet high
in front of the cape with barn attached.
Not as snow bound as Whittier's poem,
still it was best to walk to post office and church.
"Snow for Sale" the retired pharmacist advertised.
Inside, his wife, who listened to all, read pondering.

I think about that winter, pondering
how people rise to thoughts on high,
and humanity's goodness advertised
by each and every one staying attached
to community and to the village church
or bonding, reading the Bible or a poem.

The minister's wife came to call with her poem
for the pharmacist's wife skilled in pondering.
A trustee dropped by, representing the church,
to report fuel prices rising sky high
and the parsonage roof not quite attached.
"Best to seek bids," he advertised.

He emphasized that he advertised.
He preferred reports but read the poem,
contraries of budgets and spirit, notes attached.
Wise woman and educator kept pondering,
understanding yearnings for spiritual high
with grace completing nature and church.

A welcoming, inclusive, open church
a deacon deeply wished advertised.
He walked through pristine drifts piled high.
Listening to the minister's wife's poem
left him silently, questioning and pondering
how God and mammon are attached?

The minister to his flock attached,
stopped to praise in front of the church.
Affinity for snow kept him pondering.
Faith he thought best be advertised
by lives well lived and an occasional poem
to lift humanity to transcendence on high.

Wisdom on high, you are incarnate to us attached,
Like Whittier's poem, people gather, this time as church.
Love by compassion is advertised. Gracious pondering.

Endnotes

Streaming Beauty

St. John the Evangelist
Mesrop of Khizan, 1615,
Armenian, manuscript artist

illuminated a Gospel book, Isfahan,
with colors of desert and sky, sacred
art owned by the J. P. Getty Museum,

St. John is dressed in blue and green.
hues in the Old and New Testaments,
with revelatory import.

The elders of Israel saw under the
feet of God a sapphire pavement of
clearest blue, proclaiming holiness.

Mark reports that Jesus ordered people
to sit down on the green grass–in Greek
the fresh, yellow green of springtime.

The great feeding of fish and bread
gifted nourishment for body. The color
green offered hope.

Greeks did not favor blue and green,
in the Odyssey, metallic colors plus,
dawn's rosy fingers and wine-dark sea.

Not inclined to see the sky as blue
nor grass as green they found other
colors speaking, singing in their prose.

Colors in life and ancient literature
keep my mind attuned, heart pulsing,
contemplating St. John for decades.

Swirling curls envelope the Evangelist.
Blue rays flow into St. John's mouth.
His scribe, a child, is filled with wonder.

Likewise at age three I was amazed,
comforted by light shining through
cobalt vases as my mother was dying.

Vision of the Logos in streams of blue,
transcendence through light and color,
sustaining beauty, luminous Word.

Links:
"Saint John the Evangelist," by Mesrop of Khizan (Armenian, active 1605–51), 1615. From Wikimedia Commons, the free media repository. https://commons.wikimedia.org/wiki/File:Mesrop_of_Khizan_(Armenian,_active_1605_-_1651)_-_Saint_John_the_Evangelist_-_Google_Art_Project.jpg

Blue Heights

A day of beauty and blue,
Lake Moraine with mountain heights,
blue like a satin ribbon
weaves throughout my life
from the beaching of birth
to sight of the opposite shore.

My first mother sailed towards that shore.
Light shone for me through vases of blue.
At age three, life gave me artistic birth.
Color comfort bloomed, growing to heights.
Beauty and light nurtured new life,
tied together with a blue satin ribbon.

Company of blue gifts courage with a ribbon.
Writers aware of that opposite shore
with words from contemplation celebrate life:
Dante's lovely Beatrice in heaven's blue,
"Indigo buntings" in Millay's poetic heights.*
Gerard Manley Hopkins's bluebells spring birth.

---

* Edna St. Vincent Millay's unfinished poem:

> "Never before, perhaps, was such a sight—
> Only one sky (my breath!) and all that blue—
>
> Lapis and Sevres, and borage—every hue
> Of blue-jay—indigo bunting—bluebirds' flight."

The unfinished poem was published in the book *The Indigo Bunting: A Memoir of Edna St. Vincent Millay*, by Vincent Sheean, published by Schocken Books (New York) in 1973 (latest copyright, 1951, by Vincent Sheean). These couplets are on page 31. This book was found in the library of my second mother after her death.

Beauty gestates into healing, spiritual birth.
Over and under the writer weaves the ribbon.
Hopkins's bluebells in Alpine meadow heights,
Millay's unfinished poem as she drifted to the shore,
Lucy Larcom's Atlantic "strip of blue",
words culled from her Beverly hometown life.

Saving beauty transforms broken selves into life.
When Ellie, my second mother, died there was birth
with proof or temporal ambiguity from buntings blue.
A message came echoing all presents with a ribbon,
perhaps a sign from a transcendent shore
of divine love known in ineffable heights.

Ellie's sister feared Ellie would not reach heavenly heights.
I asked Ellie for two indigo buntings, a sign of life
as assurance she reached God's welcoming shore,
two buntings after her death to seal hope's birth.
Two buntings came on a sympathy card. The ribbon
of on-going life strung together images of blue.

Beauty and blue lift my eyes to mountain heights,
weave a ribbon softening hard edges of life.
Blessings give birth with grace from glory's shore.

Pandemic Peace

Cloistered by the pandemic
and by my temperament

there is strength from silence
solace in quiet.

Be still and know
that God is God.

Wordless prayer is enough:
reverence without clutter.

I paint stillness,
the calm of the mountains,

still waters of ebb tide pools,
the retreat of my life

until the deepest silence
of darkness or of light?

Connection of Presence

An ancient benediction
blooms anew as greeting.

Original context of suspicion
flowers as peace-filled trust.

Greetings! "While we are
absent one from another."
Not alone in knowing
nature can be cruel.

Not alone in this pandemic
practicing safety distance.
Not alone in shared hope
for saving sustenance.

Not alone in belief that
transcendent good will is.

Not alone.

> This poem is based on an embedded covenant-verse or benediction-poem in the Old Testament. Types are fluid and multifaceted. The narrative context is the story of Laban and Jacob making a covenant because they were not sure if they trusted each other (Gen 31:43-55).
>
> Laban said, "This heap is a witness between you and me today." Therefore he called it Galeed, and the pillar Mizpah, for he said, "The Lord watch between you and me, when we are absent one from the other." (Gen 31:48–49 NRSV)

Witness

Were you there, seeing in high
definition, when insurgents
stormed the Capitol intent on
execution?

Were you glued to your TV
like barnacles to rocks
as video clips piled into
putrid impasto?

Were you celebrating democracy,
relieved when President Biden
and Vice President Harris
took the highest oath of office
to defend the Constitution?

When fireworks burst into light,
when hope rose from the grave,
were you there?

Open Letter of Questions

Spring, 2021

Dear President Biden
and President Putin:
President Putin
and President Biden:

Call me naïve,
but please consider.

What would it take
to bring you together
on the brink of beauty
so deep you wonder at
the wonder of it all?

Would experiencing mystical
union with the Universe shape
bridge-building questions?

Some American would like
to ask, what is at stake in
maintaining Soviet authority?

I imagine Russian patriots
questioning why do you
Americans value democracy?

Common ground inquiry is:
How is the weather where
you live?

As ice thaws, do spring flowers
bloom in your land?

> Sharon R. Chace
> Poet Laureate of
> Rockport, Massachusetts
> United States of America

Pandemic Puzzle

February, 2021

Why does the Albion College
plush dog in the online book store
attract me deeply?

At age 76, I do not need another
dust collector, so why purchase?
Why? A puzzlement.

Finally I understand. This puppy
reminds me of a friendly, visiting
dog from decades past.

In junior high a gentle beagle, who
lived on the corner of Haven and
Phillips Avenues, came to play.

We rolled together in the snow,
my only fun, physical activity,
respite from all things gym.

I called him, "Friend Dog."
Now in my imagination, he barks:
"Rockport can feel friendly."

Japanese Gardens

Portland, Oregon, 2014

Water, rocks, plants,
the sacred three of
the Japanese Garden
remind me of my
miniature childhood
garden in a round,
white bowl.
I am the girl of nine
seeing the world in
bits of moss.
I am the high school girl
with her head in the heavens.
I am the college woman
discovering haiku.
I am the young mother
walking with my daughter
among the cherry blossoms.
I am a woman of seventy
connecting the stepping stones.

Cape Ann and Beyond the Cut Bridge: Culling and Cart-wheeling
Resource Publications, 2015
An Imprint of Wipf and Stock Publishers

Distillation

*A found poem in a letter
from Doris Brainard to me
Walpole, New Hampshire, October 1, 2000*

Summer has gone.
Leaves are beginning to show color.

Went apple picking
with the Dodds,
new to town,
since you were here.
I wanted to do it once more.

Tomorrow night, I will go
to a church supper in Cornish.
The menu is always pot roast.
Delicious.

I am sending you a book.*
You might find it interesting
and a bit unusual.

The usual village happenings go on:
real estate changes, sickness,
people moving in and out.

---

* *2000 Years Since Bethlehem: Images of Christ through the Centuries*, compiled by Janice T. Grana (Upper Room Books).

The town hall remodeling
progresses slowly.

There is a new Unitarian minister,
a man.

Time goes by.

Dead Whale

A Pantoum of 2012

Reverent feelings for the whale
People gathered like a vigil visiting.
Boston to Cogswell path to Cape Hedge
Skeleton will find sanctuary in New Hampshire.

People gathered like a vigil visiting.
The ocean gave him up.
Skeleton will find sanctuary in New Hampshire.
Rest as sacred remains renew regard.

The ocean gave him up.
Boston to Cogswell path to Cape Hedge
Rest as sacred remains renew regard.
Reverent feelings for the whale.

Cape Ann and Beyond the Cut Bridge: Culling and Cart-wheeling
Resource Publications, 2015
An Imprint of Wipf and Stock Publishers

Moving On

A Pantoum of 2018

Reverent feelings for the whale deepen.
Soundings echo in human hearts
Like waves reaching further on incoming tide.
Boston to Rockport to Knox College, Illinois.

Soundings echo in human hearts.
Scientists and artists unite to restore bones.
Boston to Rockport to Knox College, Illinois
Natural history preservation is celebration of creation.

Scientists and artists unite to restore bones.
Like waves reaching further on incoming tide,
Natural history preservation is celebration of creation.
Reverent feelings for the whale deepen.

Lament and Praise

I want to hold the world in my hands
Like the image of God in the folk hymn
To hold in the mind is to bless
The earth, its people, plants, animals.

Like the image of God in the folk hymn
Lifting up the globe is protest and peace
The earth, its people, plants, animals,
Mountains, seas, all creatures of the deep.

Lifting up the globe is protest and peace
To hold in the mind is to bless
Mountains, seas, all creatures of the deep
I want to hold the world in my hands.

A Memorial Poem

Sigrid Elizabeth Olson Lindo
September 12, 1945—July 21, 2020

Hallelujah chorus triumphs throughout life
Singing in the chapel choir at age nine
Senior choir, First Congregational Church, Rockport
Wife, mother, musician, artist, fundraiser.

Singing in the chapel choir at age nine
Riding logs, catching frogs—pits of Pigeon Cove
Wife, mother, musician, artist, fundraiser
Shining in Kent Place School and Wellesley College.

Riding logs, catching frogs—pits of Pigeon Cove
Senior choir, First Congregational Church, Rockport
Shining in Kent Place School and Wellesley College
Hallelujah chorus triumphs throughout life.

Author's Note: Cape Ann's granite quarrying industry created numerous "pits" and swimming holes favored by locals

Image of Life

Two
sisters
together,
Ina, Doris.
Older Ina puts
Doris through college days.
Years later the pastor of
the town's Congregational Church
sees Doris and Ina sisterly
walking around the Walpole Common, bright
sunlight blessing their day with good cheer, grace, hope.
In the nursing home the pastor finds Ina dead.
Sorrow's path starts on the road home to Colebrook and God.
Affirming life, Doris proclaims, "Joy comes with the morning."[*]
Forty years plus pass. The minister finds sunlight memory
stronger than dark sorrow of death, learning from Doris and Ina.

[*] Based on Psalm 30:5.

Fog

Fog floats down the street
in a parade of puffs.

The sun tries to break through
like happy moments

like refreshing memories
rising to awareness

in the misty isness
of the elderly man

still puffing with
the breath of life.

Fog Repeats

Deeply settled fog
off Onset.

Off Onset
deeply settled fog.

Settled fog stretches
Cape Cod to Cape Ann.

Cape Cod to Cape Ann
settled fog stretches.

Different shade of gray
not as many as in life.

Not as many as in life
different shades of gray.

Churning waves unsettle.
Chaos, universal condition.

Chaos, universal condition
churning waves unsettle.

Deeply settled fog
off Onset.

Completion

The old man hugging
his pumpkin slumps
against the door frame.
He reaches for his wife's
hand. Regaining balance,
he gives her the grandest
gift of their garden, orange
embers of glowing love
in the fullness of time.

Seasoning

Sun yellow bursting
into flame, settles
into red embers,
rose hips, saturated
hue of mature love.

In December light,
one seaside rose
is a last blooming
awaiting the frost
in front of mystery

This poem is a syllabic poem. I learned about this form in the book *Creating Poetry* by John Drury. The concept requires one to write a poem in lines that alternate with uneven numbers. I chose 7 ... 5. Even numbers sound too much like iambic pentameter. In this kind of poetry it is okay to end a line with a preposition or conjunction, or even to hyphenate words to maintain the syllable count.

Shoots

August, 2020

The next generation of
rose of Sharon trees
volunteered from up the street.
Granite stones, white blooms
hard and soft, old and new blend.

Pink rose of Sharon
peaked in two thousand sixteen.
College reunion—
Fifty years flowed by with rush.

Like me the old trees
start to wane but still bloom bright.
Past studies and fresh
thoughts converge in artistry.
Whatever life brings
gratitude rises within.

Intimations

"Which house is yours?"
asked my new friend,
giving me a ride home,
after the women's group
discussion about passages
of life: Fording quiet
streams and crossing
roaring rivers.

"Where the yellow flowers are."

The black-eyed Susans
the bright marigolds,
the evening primroses
vying for attention with
the Montauk daisies that will
not bud until October.

Savoring beauty is saving now.

If there is life in gardens
beyond, I will bloom at home
where the yellow flowers are.

Sinatra Inspired

"Parsons, what are you doing?"
my college swimming professor
barked at me using my maiden
name as was the custom.
Avoiding sophomoric sarcasm,
yet asserting myself, I replied:
"Doing as it is written in the Bible,
never let your left hand know what
the right hand is doing.'" Hoping for
the best I added, "Surely someone in
twelve years of Rockport education
noticed that this sort of thing is hard
for me. Why not check my records in
the admission office?"

She did. Next class sweet as
the sticky buns my friends and
I savored.
Reports must have stuck!
"Looks like that is a good way for
you to swim!"

Fast forward to graduation: My advisor
said to my family, "This was very hard
for Sharon, do you think it was worth it?"
I do not remember their answers but
noted the pause for thought.

In the years ahead there would be days of
smooth sailing and rough seas.
Through all kinds of weather,
on shore winds or summer breezes,
I sail my own barque.

Clothing and Callings

The time is coming when
I will not need one more
pair of pink sneakers,
another dainty bow blouse,
a poem to pen nor a note
to send.

The markers of my life matter
and so do yours.

Translation

The social worker called,
"It is time to consider
hospice care for your
husband's mom."
Directed by an existential
imperative to translate
biology into theology,
I made a mental note,
a post in my mind
to memorize by rote.
The skin is breaking down
means, *Dissolving into God.*

Portfolio of Painterly Poems: A Pilgrim's Path to God
Resource Publications, 2006
An Imprint of Wipf and Stock Publishers

Meet Me

A love poem

Two cart shopping day.

You take this one.
I'll fetch my cart.

Potatoes,
Rice pilaf,

Beefsteak,
Yogurt,

Meet me at the ice cream.

Two carts passing in the craft aisle:

Graph paper,
Watercolor rough,

Look: A tiny calculator.
Remember slide rulers?
Never mastered them,
Gave mine away,

Study CAD drawings,
Contemplate Jackson Pollock,

Meet me at the ice cream.

Blissful oblivion,
Rest in God,

Sweet dessert,
Sweet dessert,

Meet Me.

Indigo Bunting Sonnet

Two weeks before Eleanor Parsons died
I asked her for a sign from the Beyond
Specifying two indigo buntings
Loveliest birds, pure notes of heaven's song.
Two birds don't have to be in the same place.
Just one would seem like a coincidence.
Double sightings would make a stronger case,
Confirm God's wide welcome, love's deepest sense.
Before the memorial service day
A blessed sympathy note came in the mail
An indigo bunting: "Thank you." I prayed.
Bunting also on the back, my spirit sailed.
Proof or temporal ambiguity
Creating room for beauty's mystery?

Cape Ann and Beyond the Cut Bridge: Culling and Cart-wheeling
Resource Publications, 2015
An Imprint of Wipf and Stock Publishers

Blue Sonnet

Blue morning glories reach from ground to sky,
Jacob's ladder connecting earth, heaven.
Singing, angel muse patiently stands by.
Pure hue, glory, loveliness is leaven.
Hagar looking upon the face of God
Lived. So shall those whose gaze is strong enough
To embrace the icon nourished in sod.
Beauty so deep sadness is joyful hush.
Fathers of Israel saw beneath God's feet
A sapphire pavement. Hallow, praise, chant.
Sing in Heaven's City evil's defeat.
Foundations of treasured, precious blue stone,
Power, purest presence, God's face alone.

Author's Note: The cover painting on *Portfolio of Painterly Poems*, my watercolor collage based on Exodus 24:9–10, is the companion art to this poem. The elders/fathers of Israel climb a mountain and see a sapphire pavement under the feet of God. God can be a focal point, as I represented with a single red dot.

Portfolio of Painterly Poems: A Pilgrim's Path to God
Resource Publications, 2006
An Imprint of Wipf and Stock Publishers

Goodwill Dawning

Wishing you many
rose madder mornings,
deepest peony pink,
with russet streaks,
not red enough to be a sign
that "Sailors take warning."

Instead, Good morning!
Homer's gentle "rosy fingers,"
sky sign, across centuries
announces the dawning day,
like good wishes, kind regards
signaling that life can be friendly,
rose madder softening hard edges.

Imperative

A boy about eight years old to his parents
who were taking pictures from the top of
Sulphur Mountain in Banff National Park,
Canada;
"Never delete the rainbow.
Never delete the rainbow."

Thank you to the young boy with his sight and insight.

Previously published in:
Cape Ann and Beyond the Cut Bridge: Culling and Cart-wheeling
Resource Publications, 2015
An Imprint of Wipf and Stock Publishers

Unlocking the Word An Anthology of Found Poetry
Edited by Jonas Zdanys
Literary Press, Lamar University, 2018

Appendix A
Padraic Colum Evokes Gratitude

SELDOM, IF EVER, HAS A POEM struck me on a first reading with as much import as did Padraic Colum's "An Old Woman of the Roads." Unlike the unnamed woman in the poem who *longed* to have a little house, my husband and I actually own a little house. This old woman summons me to deeper thanksgiving and reminds me of a conversation with my English professor during Albion College days in the 1960s. You can find the entire poem online at www.poemhunter.com.

I feel at home in our tiny house and enjoy using my splatterware dishes and pans, especially the blue and white ones. I do not dust my porcelain cat collection as much as I did in sixth grade when weekly dusting was a new-found skill.

When Elsie Munro, many students' favorite English professor, told me more than fifty years ago that she did not like weekly dusting, I told her about my cat collection. I suggested that perhaps by dusting her pretty things she could more fully enjoy them. She thanked me and said that helped.

In retrospect I wished I had asked her to tell me more about her treasures. Only recently I realized that the material and the spiritual are not always far apart. My family was not materialistic, so gifts other than for birthdays or Christmas are noteworthy. My favorite porcelain cat is tiny—a surprise gift *just because* from my second mother, Ellie, who raised me after my first mother died when I was three and a half. Material objects such as that tiny cat can represent aspects of selves or speak of deepest yearnings. My precious cat holds a blue ball. In a pottery class with other sixth-grade Girl Scouts, I made a black cat holding a blue ball. I have always displayed this larger black cat and the small white and black

Appendix A

cat together. This arrangement suggests both ongoing childhood grief for mother loss and also yearnings for connection to both my first mother and to Ellie. Those connections unfolded over a lifetime. My mother was a librarian and fine painter in oils. I still do watercolors with the same colors my mother used. Ellie was the first kindergarten teacher in Rockport and later was most noted for her books about Rockport.

I've published a story/coloring book titled *Sycamore's First Poem*. I wrote the story, and my daughter Amy, who is playful like my first mother, illustrated it. Sycamore is a calico cat that meanders around town and then writes her first poem. Honored to be the poet laureate of Rockport, I want to serve people with poetry, which is why I wrote a book that is primarily for first graders—it is my way of teaching like Ellie and contributing to the children's room in the Rockport Library like my first mother. Like my mother Katharine, I paint. Like Ellie, I write. Double legacies are a lasting grace. Immersed in blessings, I offer gratitude.

I remind myself to enjoy the treasures of our household but remember to avoid collecting more! However, a blue and white speckled cat did catch my attention the other day. Admiration only . . . did not buy. Better still, my husband, Ernest, bought me two calico cats for my collection. When the time comes to pass along my figurines, the cats will be happy memories as they go on their way.

Author's Note: This essay, now with minor edits, was first published by Christians in the Visual Arts (CIVA) and republished with their enthusiastic permission by *The Gloucester Daily Times*, issue of October 2, 2020.

www.ingramcontent.com/pod-product-compliance
Lightning Source LLC
LaVergne TN
LVHW021549080426
835510LV00019B/2452